Jesus

Is Lord Of...

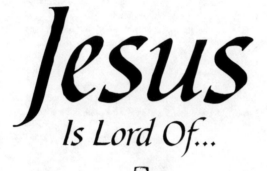

Alma Pugh

WESTBOW
PRESS®
A DIVISION OF THOMAS NELSON
& ZONDERVAN

Scripture taken from the King James Version of the Bible.

NKJV: Scripture taken from the New King James Version®. Copyright © 1982 by Thomas Nelson. Used by permission. All rights reserved.

WestBow Press books may be ordered through booksellers or by contacting:

WestBow Press
A Division of Thomas Nelson & Zondervan
1663 Liberty Drive
Bloomington, IN 47403
www.westbowpress.com
1 (866) 928-1240

ISBN: 978-1-5127-9148-8 (sc)
ISBN: 978-1-5127-9147-1 (e)

Print information available on the last page.

WestBow Press rev. date: 07/15/2017

Jesus is the Lord of Abundance

He is our El-Shaddi-The Lord that is more than enough.

St. John 10:10

The Thief (Satan, that old devil) cometh not but to steal, and kill, and to destroy.

I am (Jesus) com that they (you, me and all that believe in the I am) might have life(Zoe) and that they might have it more abundantly.

2 Corinthians 9: 8-11

And God is able to make all grace abound toward you; that ye, always having all sufficiency in all things, may abound to every good work:

(As it is written, He hath dispersed abroad; he hath given to the poor: his righteousness remaineth forever.

Now he that ministereth seed to the sower both minister bread for your food, and multiply your seed sown, and increase the fruits of your righteousness;)

Being enriched in everything to all bountifulness, which causeth through us thanksgiving to God.

2 Corinthians 8-11 Message Bible

8-11 God can pour on the blessings in astonishing ways so that you're ready for anything and everything, more than just ready to do what needs to be done. As one psalmist puts it,

> He throws caution to the winds,
> giving to the needy in reckless abandon.
> His right-living, right-giving ways
> never run out, never wear out.

This most generous God who gives seed to the farmer that becomes bread for your meals is more than extravagant with you. He gives you something you can then give away, which grows into full-formed lives, robust in God, wealthy in every way, so that you can be generous in every way, producing with us great praise to God.

I remember the time when I was praying for another job. I had been with this agency for fifteen years. They were good years. I will go as far as to say they were great years but I wanted something different. Something more and new. I asked God to give me another job with a pay increase and less responsibility.

Let me tell you God did just that. He didn't move me from the agency, instead He open a new position within the same agency. I applied and got everything that I had asked Him for. Now I'm able to give and do more for the Kingdom of God. Praise God.

Ephesians 3:20-21

Now unto him that is able to do exceeding **abundantly** above all that we ask or think, according to the power that worketh in us,[21] Unto him be glory in the church by Christ Jesus throughout all ages, world without end. Amen.

He has no respect of person. He is the Lord of Abundance. We can Ask It! We can Think It! He will Do It! He's our most generous God. Amen

Lord Jesus we thank you for being The Lord of Abundance. We receive and embrace all that you have for us. In Jesus' Name Amen.

Jesus is the Lord of Benefits

Psalm 68:19

Blessed be the Lord, who daily loadeth us with benefits, even the God of our salvation. Selah.

Psalm 103: 1-2

Bless the Lord, O my soul: and all that is within me, bless his holy name.

Bless the Lord, O my soul, and forget not all his benefits:

The Psalmist David commands his soul to Bless the Lord and forget not **all** His benefits.

Benefits:

1. Who forgiveth all thine iniquities.
2. Who healeth all thy diseases.
3. Who redeemeth thy life from destruction.
4. Who crowneth thee with loving kindness and tender mercies.

5. Who satisfieth thy mouth with good things; so that thy youth is renewed like the eagle's.

These are just a few of the benefits. If you are like me I receive and embrace **All** that Jesus has shed His blood for me to have. Amen and Amen.

Jesus is The Lord of the Breakthrough (Jehovah Perazim)

2 Samuel 5:17-20

Now when the Philistines heard that they had anointed David king over Israel, all the Philistines went up to search for David. And David heard of it and went down to the stronghold. 18 The Philistines also went and deployed themselves in the Valley of Rephaim. So David inquired of the Lord, saying, "Shall I go up against the Philistines? Will You deliver them into my hand?"

And the Lord said to David, "Go up, for I will doubtless deliver the Philistines into your hand."

So David went to Baal Perazim, and David defeated them there; and he said, "The Lord has broken through my enemies before me, like a breakthrough of water." Therefore, he called the name of that place Baal Perazim (Literally Master of Breakthroughs)

In this passage we see where the enemies were coming against The Lord's anointed. David knew that God was with him. The scripture said that David heard about and went down into a stronghold (a place that has been fortified so as to protect it against attack) David used this place as an opportunity to pray because the next time the text speaks of David he was inquiring of the Lord as to what to do and asking the Lord to deliver his enemies into his hands. Which God did in a mighty way.

God did not run out of breakthroughs when He defeated David's enemies or when Paul and Silas were in a Roman's prison.

Acts 16:25-26

And at midnight Paul and Silas prayed, and sang praises unto God: and the prisoners heard them.

And suddenly there was a great earthquake, so that the foundations of the prison were shaken: and immediately all the doors were opened, and every one's bands were loosed.

He's the Lord of Breakthroughs. Let us pray and ask God what it is He wants us to do. He will give us clear guidance just as He did David. He may tell us to pursue or he may tell us just do as Paul and Silas did pray and sing. Either way we have the victory. Because he is the Lord of all our breakthroughs. Glory be to God. Amen!

Just as He was with David, Paul and Silas so is He with every believer that believeth in Him. There is nothing that is opposing God's Anointed that Jesus hasn't defeated on the cross with His Blood.

Corinthians 15:57

But thanks be to God, which giveth us the victory through our Lord Jesus Christ. Amen.

Jesus is Lord of Compassion:

Compassion- Base on the Latin root of the word, the meaning of compassion is to suffer with. The meaning of compassion is to recognize the suffering of others then take action to help.

Psalms 86:15

But thou, O Lord, art a God full of compassion, and gracious, longsuffering, and plenteous in mercy and truth.

Lamentations 3:22

It is of the LORD'S mercies that we are not consumed, because his compassions fail not.

Micah 7:19

He will turn again, he will have compassion upon us; he will subdue our iniquities; and thou wilt cast all their sins into the depths of the sea.

Matthew 9:36

But when he (**JESUS**) saw the multitudes, he was moved with compassion on them, because they fainted, and were scattered abroad, as sheep having no shepherd.

Matthew 14:14

"And Jesus went forth, and saw a great multitude, and was moved with compassion toward them, and he healed their sick."

Mark 1:41

And Jesus, moved with compassion, put forth his hand, and touched him, and saith unto him, I will; be thou clean.

Luke 7:13

And when the Lord saw her, he had compassion on her, and said unto her, Weep not.

Wow. Jesus is Lord of Compassion. He feels what we feel and not only that He is willing and able to help us. Thank you Lord. You are so amazing. I love you.

Jesus is the Lord of Counsel

Counsel-

1. To give advice or deliberate opinion to another for the government of his conduct; to advise.
2. The will of God or his truth and doctrines concerning the way of salvation
3. Directions of God's word.

Psalm 33:10–11

The Lord bringeth the counsel of the heathen to nought: he maketh the devices of the people of none effect.

The counsel of the Lord standeth for ever, the thoughts of his heart to all generations.

Psalm 73:24

Thou shalt guide me with thy counsel, and afterward receive me to glory.

Isaiah 28:29

This also cometh forth from the Lord of hosts, which is wonderful in **counsel,** and excellent in working.

John 14:26

But the Comforter, which is the Holy Ghost, whom the Father will send in my name, he shall teach you all things, and bring all things to your remembrance, whatsoever I have said unto you.

People of God we need the Lord of Counsel and the counsel of our Lord in our everyday life. We need the Holy Spirit which is the Spirit of Truth. It is He that keeps us from error. Now this doesn't mean that we will not make mistakes. It means we do not have to be gullible or ignorant to Satan schemes and devices. If we are going to be keen concerning these last days, we must have God's Spirit living on the inside of us to lead and guide us into the Truth.

ST. John 14:16

And I will pray the Father, and he shall give you another **Comforter,** that he may abide with you for ever;

In other bible translations He the Comforter, the Holy Spirit, the Strengthener, and **Counselor**.

He is within us the believers to give us wisdom, direction, understanding and to help us in every area of our lives. Praise God.

God has also given gifts to His body (Ephesians 4: 8-11)

Men and Women that are filled with His Spirit to give us Godly Counsel.

His Word, the Holy Scriptures, the Bible is also our relevant counsel for today.

Father in the Name of Jesus we embrace, receive and obey your wonderful counsel that comes from your Spirit, Your Word and Your people. In Jesus Name Amen.

Jesus is Lord of Deliverance/ Salvation:

Deliverance is defined as a rescue from bondage or danger, to save from, to set free.

Jesus has rescued us from the bondage and dangers of sin through the shedding of His atoning blood on Calvary's Cross.

St. John 3:16-17

For God so loved the world, that he gave his only begotten Son, that whosoever believeth in him should not perish, but have everlasting life.

For God sent not his Son into the world to condemn the world; but that the world through him might be saved.

When we believe that God sent his only begotten Son (Jesus) the perfect lamb. The only sacrifice we will ever need to wash us completely and finally from any/all sin past, present and future.

We are made free. We are made righteous. We are delivered from all eternal punishment of sin.

Romans 6:23

For the wages of sin is death; **but the gift of God is eternal life through Jesus Christ our Lord.**

Colossians 1:13

Who hath delivered us from the power of darkness, and hath translated us into the kingdom of his dear Son:

We are delivered from all the powers of darkness and are now in the Kingdom of His Dear Son.

Jesus has also delivered unto us what is in His kingdom.

Righteousness, Peace and Joy in the Holy Ghost. (Romans 14:17) Hallelujah Amen

We do not have to be sin conscience. We are God conscience, Jesus conscience and Holy Spirit Conscience. Amen.

Let's take a look at 2 Peter 2:9

The Lord knoweth how to **deliver** the godly out of temptations, and to reserve the unjust unto the day of judgment to be punished:

The Lord also will **deliver** us from temptations. He's a God like that.

Sometime our deliverance from trials doesn't manifest in the time we desire or think it should. **(ALTHOUGH ALL OUR DELIVERENCE IS ALREADY DONE IN JESUS)**

It is those times He is the Lord our Sustainer and our Ability.

1 Corinthians 10:13

There hath no temptation taken you but such as is common to man: **but God is faithful,** who will not suffer you to be tempted above that ye are able; but will with the temptation also make a way to escape, that ye may be able to bear it.

Jesus is Lord of Everlasting Strength:

Isaiah 26:4

Trust ye in the Lord forever: for in the Lord Jehovah is everlasting strength:

Jesus is our strength. Let's us total rely and depend upon Him.

When we are weak he is our strength that will last forever. Amen.

Jesus is Lord of Forgiveness:

2 Corinthians 5:17

Therefore, if any man be in Christ, he is a new creature: old things are passed away; behold, all things are become new.

Ephesians 1:3-9

Blessed be the God and Father of our Lord Jesus Christ, who hath blessed us with all spiritual blessings in heavenly places in Christ:

According as he hath chosen us in him before the foundation of the world, **that we should be holy and without blame before him in love:**

Having predestinated us unto the adoption of children by Jesus Christ to himself, according to the good pleasure of his will,

To the praise of the glory of his grace, wherein he hath made us accepted in the beloved.

In whom we have redemption through his blood, **the forgiveness of sins, according to the riches of his grace;**

Wherein he hath abounded toward us in all wisdom and prudence;

Having made known unto us the mystery of his will, according to his good pleasure which he hath purposed in himself:

Hebrews 10:17

And their sins and iniquities will I remember no more.

When we receive Jesus into our hearts he forgives us. We may not feel any different and the devil wants to use our feelings to deceive us.

It's not by our feelings that we are forgiven. It's by us believing in the Blood of Jesus.

We are New in Him. Our sins are all forgiven. Amen. Thank you Jesus.

Jesus is Lord of Freedom:

John 8:32 And ye shall know the truth, and the truth shall make you free.

Jesus is the truth. He's not a version of a truth. Jesus is the whole truth and nothing but the truth because he is the Son of the True and Living God.

When we continue to grow in knowing Jesus (not knowing of Jesus) who is the Truth, we become free from bias, perceptions, carnal -fleshly mindedness, sin consciousness, religion, tradition of men etc.

John 8:36 If the Son therefore shall make you free, ye shall be free indeed.

When Jesus makes us free. We were Free. We do not have to be entangled any more with that yoke of bondage. Hallelujah! Amen.

Galatians 5:1 Stand fast therefore in the liberty(freedom) wherewith Christ hath made us free, and be not entangled again with the yoke of bondage.

We are believers in the finish works of Jesus. We will not be moved. We know in whom we believe. We are free in Jesus. Amen and Amen.

Jesus is Lord of Goodness:

Psalm 27:13

I had fainted, unless I had believed to see **the goodness of the Lord** in the land of the living.

Wow! This verse. There is goodness in the land of the living. It's found in Jesus the Lord of goodness. Things are happening all around us that are not good, but when we focus on Jesus, His word and His ways. We can say like David the author of Psalm 27. I will not faint because I'm focusing on the goodness of the Lord.

Psalm 135:3

Praise the Lord; for the Lord is good: sing praises unto his name; for it is pleasant.

Psalm 65:11

Thy crownest the year with your goodness; and thy paths drop fatness

Hebrews 9:11-12

But Christ being come an high priest of good things to come, by a greater and more perfect tabernacle, not made with hands, that is to say, not of this building;

Neither by the blood of goats and calves, but by his own blood he entered in once into the holy place, having obtained eternal redemption for us.

Jesus is So Good to Us, So Good! He is the Lord of Goodness!

Jesus is Lord of Glory

The word 'glory' is a noun, a word for high renown or honor; a word for magnificence or great beauty; a word for a person, place or thing

The word 'glory' is also a verb meaning to take great pride or pleasure in.

Hebrews 1:1-3

God, who at sundry times and in divers manners spake in time past unto the fathers by the prophets,

Hath in these last days spoken unto us by his Son, whom he hath appointed heir of all things, by whom also he made the worlds;

Who being the brightness of his glory, and the express image of his person, and upholding all things by the word of his power, when he had by himself purged our sins, sat down on the right hand of the Majesty on high:

2 Corinthians 3:18

But we all, with open face beholding as in a glass **the glory of the Lord**, are changed into the same image from glory to glory, even as by the Spirit of the Lord.

People of God we are being transformed into the very same Glory that is Jesus by the Spirit of the Lord of Glory.

Habakkuk 2:14

Declares for the earth shall be filled with the knowledge of the glory of the Lord, as the waters cover the sea.

The Prophet Habakkuk is not only speaking about this planet being filled with the knowledge of the glory of God but he is also prophesying that we the believers (Earthen vessels that houses the Holy Spirit) will know that Glory. We will express and declare that glory in the earth. We will be transporters of that heavenly glory. Amen.

We are being changed from glory to glory by the Lord of the Glory. O my God how awesome. Praise God! Hallelujah!

Jesus is Lord of Grace: (from the Greek New Testament word Charis) It focus on the provision of Salvation

Grace is God's unmerited favor. It is kindness from God that we don't deserve. There is nothing we have done, nor can ever do to earn this favor. It is a gift from God in the Person of Jesus.

Grace is divine assistance from God to do and accomplish those things which he has assigned to us in the earth. I like what one minister said He has poured His Super on our natural so that we are His Super Natural beings in the earth to get His will done. Amen

John 1:17

For the law was given by Moses, but Grace and Truth came by Jesus Christ.

Ephesians 2:8-9

For by grace (His unmerited favor) are ye saved through faith; and that not of yourselves: it is the gift of God:

Not of works, lest any man should boast.

We were not able to keep the laws that was given to Moses.

Romans 5 :1-2

Therefore, being justified by faith, we have peace with God through our Lord Jesus Christ:

By whom also we have access by faith into **this grace** wherein we stand, and rejoice in hope of the glory of God.

It was not because of anything that we did or did not do. It is because of God Grace's. His unmerited favor towards us, that he sent his only begotten Son to die. Now that we believe in Him(Jesus) who is Grace and true we are no longer under the law of bondage but we are walking in the Grace of God.

Thank you Jesus for being the Lord of Grace.

John 1:14

And the Word was made flesh, and dwelt among us, (and we beheld his glory, the glory as of the only begotten of the Father,) full of grace and truth.

The Word(Jesus) became flesh and made his dwelling among us. We have seen his glory, the glory of the one and only Son, who came from the Father, full of Grace and Truth.

Jesus is Lord of Healing:

Isaiah 53:4-5

Surely he(Jesus) hath borne our griefs, and carried our sorrows: yet we did esteem him stricken, smitten of God, and afflicted.

But he was wounded for our transgressions, he was bruised for our iniquities: the chastisement of our peace was upon him; and with his stripes **we are healed.**

1 Peter 2:24

"Who His own self bare our sins in his own body on the tree, that we, being dead to sins, should live unto righteousness: by whose stripes **ye were healed**."

Surely (of the truth) We were healed over two-thousand years ago. When Jesus was crucified all our healing, I said all our healing emotional, spiritual, physical, and financial was completed when Jesus said it is finished.

We are not trying to get healed. **WE ARE HEAL**. Declare it! Speak it out into the atmosphere.

I thank you Jesus who is Lord of healing; for manifesting your healing in everyone that is reading this book. I declare healing in every area; spiritual, emotional, physical and yes financial because of your precious, powerful, atoning, restoring, renewing blood. To You be all Glory and Praise throughout all the Age. World without end. It is so. Amen.

Jesus is Lord of the Harvest:

Genesis 8:22

"While the earth remaineth, seedtime and harvest, and cold and heat, and summer and winter, and day and night shall not cease."

According to this scripture there will always be opportunities (a set of circumstances that makes it possible to do something) to sow.

Galatians 6:7 Be not deceived; God is not mocked: for **whatsoever** a man soweth, that shall he also reap.

A farmer does not sow apple seeds and then reap oranges. He reaps apples of course.

When love is sown, love is reaped. When kindness is sown, kindness is reaped.

When money is sown, money is reaped. Whatsoever a man soweth, that will he also reap.

Glory be to God. It's not limited to a certain few folks to be financially secure and prosperous.

It's on us dear friends. What are we sowing?

Jesus is Lord of the Harvest. He's the Overseer. He's the General. No one can stop anyone from reaping. First the Seed, then Time and next the Harvest. Hallelujah Amen the principle works.

He is also the Lord of the Harvest that will send labors to field.

Matthew 9:38 Pray ye therefore the Lord of the harvest, that he will send forth laborers into his harvest.

Jesus is Lord of Joy:

JOY, n- The passion or emotion excited by the acquisition or expectation of good;

Nehemiah 8:10

Then he said unto them, Go your way, eat the fat, and drink the sweet, and send portions unto them for whom nothing is prepared: for this day is holy unto our Lord: neither be ye sorry; **for the joy of the Lord is your strength.**

Zephaniah 3:17

The Lord thy God in the midst of thee is mighty; he will save, he will rejoice over thee with joy; he will rest in his love, he will joy over thee with singing.

I really love these passages. The Lord our God, He is in the mist of us. He's mighty to save not only that He rejoices over us with joy.

God is passionate and excited over us because he knows the good that is in Him concerning us.

He in in the mist of us, that's His goodness. He saves us. That's His goodness. Wow He rejoices over us with passion and excitement. That is why His joy gives us strength. When we embrace the Lord's Joy we can't help but to be empower and infused with His strength. My God, this is love overflowing. Thank you Jesus for being the Lord of Joy. I receive. Amen.

Jesus is Lord of Justification:

Justification- The action of declaring or making righteous in the sight of God.

Galatians 2:16

Knowing that a man is not justified by the works of the law, but by the faith of Jesus Christ, even we have believed in Jesus Christ, that we might be justified by the faith of Christ, and not by the works of the law: for by the works of the law shall no flesh be justified.

Jesus actions declared all who believes in Him are made righteous (in Right standing with the Father God)

What actions did Jesus do? He shed His blood on a criminal's cross. He died was buried in a borrowed tomb, He arose on the third day with all power and then he ascended back to heaven where He is seated at the right hand of God the Father where He ever liveth to make intercession for you and me.

One day Jesus is coming back to get us who believe in Him. Jesus is Lord of Justification. He has justified us. Glory be to God.

Jesus is Lord of Knowledge:

ST. John 1:1-3

In the beginning was the Word(JESUS), and the Word (JESUS) was with God, and the Word(JESUS) was God.

The same was in the beginning with God.

All things were made by him(JESUS); and without him(JESUS) was not anything made that was made.

Colossians 2:2 -3

That their hearts might be comforted, being knit together in love, and unto all riches of the full assurance of understanding, to the acknowledgement of the mystery of God, and of the Father, and of Christ;

In whom are hid all the treasures of wisdom and knowledge.

In Christ Jesus our Lord is Wisdom and Knowledge. It is in Him by way of the Holy Spirit that we will know the mysteries of our Father God. Thank you Jesus. Amen.

Jesus is Lord of Peace

2 Thessalonians 3:16

Now the Lord of peace himself give you peace always by all means. The Lord be with you all.

1 Thessalonians 5:23

And the very God of peace sanctify you **wholly**; and I pray God your whole spirit and soul and body be preserved blameless unto the coming of our Lord Jesus Christ.

Jesus is Jehovah-shalom-God our Peace

There is Nothing (not one thing) Broken, Nothing Lacking, Nothing Missing in Jesus' Peace. Jesus is Whole

People of God Jesus has given us that same peace. That same wholeness.

St. John 14:27

Peace I leave with you, my peace I give unto you: not as the world giveth, give I unto you. Let not your heart be troubled, neither let it be afraid.

In the opening of this chapter Jesus was talking with his disciples. The first thing he said to them is let not your hearts be troubled, believe in God, believe in me.

We are believing Believers that believe. Amen and amen. Hallelujah! Thank you Jesus!

Then we find at the latter part of this chapter Jesus is saying it again, but this time he said my peace I give you. We take His peace instead of letting our hearts be troubled.

The peace that Jesus gives us will cause us to rest in Him during any circumstance or situation in this journey called life.

When life challenges come we have been commanded to let not our hearts be troubled or afraid.

Instead **let the peace of God rule in your hearts**, to the which also ye are called in one body; and be ye thankful. Please remember to Be thankful. Being thankful and keeping our minds on the Lord of Peace(Jesus) are conduits(channels) for perfect peace. Amen

Philippians 4:7

And the peace of God, which passeth all understanding, shall keep your hearts and minds through Christ Jesus.

We have peace with God and We have the peace of God both is because of Jesus the Lord of Peace. Glory be to God! Thank you Jesus!

Jesus is Lord of Redemption:

Redemption is the English translation of the Greek word *agorazo*, meaning "to purchase in the marketplace." In ancient times, it often referred to the act of buying a slave. It carried the meaning of freeing someone from chains, prison, or slavery. Wow!

Romans 5:19

For as by one man' s(Adam) disobedience all were made sinners, so by the obedience of one shall many be made righteous. (All have the opportunity but not all will believe in the finished work of Jesus on the cross)

Adam sin against God. He then caused all mankind to be born into sin.

In the old Covenant the priest offered sacrifices (goats, calves and bulls etc.) each year for his sins and the sins of the people

Hebrews 9:22 - And almost all things are by the law purged with blood; and without shedding of blood is no remission.

We needed a redeemer. A perfect lamb. A perfect blood offering. His Name is Jesus. They hung Jesus high. He's bloody body was viewed by all in heaven, all demonic powers and those in the earth. He paid the price for our sins. All God's punishment for sin were laid on Jesus.

There is no more payment due. Thank you Jesus for being our Redeemer. Glory!

But when the Messiah(Jesus) arrived, high priest of the superior things of this new covenant, he bypassed the old tent and its trappings in this created world and went straight into heaven's "tent"—the true Holy Place—once and for all. He also bypassed the sacrifices consisting of goat and calf blood, instead using his own blood as the payment to set us free once and for all.

Glory to God! Amen and Hallelujah!

Jesus is Lord of Revelations: (Jesus is the Revelator of the book of Revelations and John is the writer.)

Revelations 1: 1-2 The Revelation of Jesus Christ, which God gave unto him, to shew unto his servants things which must shortly come to pass; and he sent and signified *it* by his angel unto his servant John:

Who bare record of the word of God, and of the testimony of Jesus Christ, and of all things that he saw.

Revelations-noun

a surprising and previously unknown fact, (Truth by the Holy Spirit) especially one that is made known in a dramatic way:

the making known of something that was previously secret or unknown:

Ephesians 1:17

That the God of our Lord Jesus Christ, the Father of glory, may give unto you the spirit of wisdom and revelation in the knowledge of him:

The Apostle Paul prayed this prayer for the saints at Ephesus. It is for us saints/ believers today. Paul wanted them and us to experience the revelations that comes from God the Father to Jesus the Son and is revealed or disclosed by the Holy Spirit.

I Corinthians 2:9-11

Please read the entire chapter

But as it is written, Eye hath not seen, nor ear heard, neither have entered into the heart of man, the things which God hath prepared for them that love him.

But God hath revealed them unto us by his Spirit: for the Spirit searcheth all things, yea, the deep things of God.

For what man knoweth the things of a man, save the spirit of man which is in him? even so the things of God knoweth no man, but the Spirit of God.

Please listen there are greater things coming to us. God has been so gracious and kind, however according to this scripture we haven't seen or heard anything yet **but He is revealing it to us by way of the Spirit of God.**

The Spirit of God gets the revelations from the Son of God (Jesus). The Son of God gets it from the Father God. Wow.

Jesus is the Lord of Revelations. He will show Himself Strong and Mighty in our lives and we can know what's coming by He the Holy Spirit.

People of God we have to embrace the total Godhead. Father, Son and Holy Spirit. Amen

Jesus is Lord of the Rest

Matthew 11:28-30

Come unto me, all ye that labour and are heavy laden, and **I will give you rest**.

Take my yoke upon you, and learn of me; for I am meek and lowly in heart: and ye shall find rest unto your souls.

For my yoke is easy, and my burden is light.

Psalm 23: 1-2

The Lord is my shepherd; I shall not want.

He maketh me to lie down in green pastures: he leadeth me beside the still waters.

Hebrews 4:3

For we which have believed do enter into rest, as he said, As I have sworn in my wrath, if they shall enter into my rest: although the works were finished from the foundation of the world.

Jesus is Lord of Righteousness

Romans 5:19

for as through the one man's disobedience the many were made sinners, even so through the obedience of the one the many will be made righteous.

The first Adam sinned by disobeying God therefore he caused all of us to enter in to sin. Then comes the Last Adam Jesus the Christ the Anointed of God. God took His righteousness for our sins. Now because we believe in the atoning work on the cross by Jesus. We are made righteous. ***Hallelujah! Thank you Lord Jesus!***

Jesus is Lord of Victory:

Psalm 44:44-7

Thou art my King, O God: command deliverances for Jacob.

Through thee will we push down our enemies: through thy name will we tread them under that rise up against us.

For I will not trust in my bow, neither shall my sword save me.

But thou hast saved us from our enemies, and hast put them to shame that hated us.

The Lord is the one that fights for us. Let us continue to rest in the Lord. He is truly on our side.

2 Corinthians 2:14

Now thanks be unto God, who always causeth us to triumph in Christ and who maketh manifest through us the savor of His knowledge in every place

Jesus is Lord of Wisdom

Luke 2:40

And the child grew, and waxed strong in spirit, filled with wisdom, and God's grace was upon him.

James 1:5

But the wisdom that is from above is first pure, then peaceable, gentle, and easy to be intreated, full of mercy and good fruits, without partiality, and without hypocrisy.

Wow Jesus is Lord of, because He is Lord period. He is the totality of all these divine attributes.

The ones that's listed and defined in this book and the one that He himself will reveal to you by way of His Spirit.

This is not the end my dear friend because the Holy Spirit will continue to make Jesus known to us. This is the will of God.

Alma Pugh

Lord we embrace the Godhead. God the Father, God the Son and God the Holy Spirit. Thank You for showing us who Christ Jesus is in us. Amen

Jesus is Lord of.........

I encourage you as you get greater revelations of who our wonderful Lord Jesus is share, Tell the glad tidings and advance the kingdom of God. Amen and Amen.

Printed in the United States
By Bookmasters